No Garden For Girls Like Me

Archives Aflame

Garima Singh

BookLeaf Publishing

India | USA | UK

Made with ❤ on the BookLeaf Publishing Platform

www.bookleafpub.in

www.bookleafpub.com

Dedication

__For my mother —__
I miss you in every line.
She raised a writer.
You're holding her words.

Preface

Life is uncertain. What we hope for may not happen —
or even exist — and for some unknown reason, that's
okay.
When things turn out for the better, we accept not
knowing. But when they turn out for the worst, we
wrestle with our minds, searching for happiness while
haunted by the weight of uncertainty.
Letting go *is easy for some.* I have never been one of
them.
And that's why, more often than not, I become the very
reason for my unhappiness —
as if the world's torment wasn't already enough.
Still, **I refuse to apologize.**
For being deeply impacted by things.
For holding on too tightly.
For choosing myself — again and again — even when it's
messy.
For being who I am, unapologetically.
*Just as the ocean never apologizes for its depth, or the
mountain for its vastness, or the night for its darkness.*
I must be the master of my fate, the captain of my soul,
and let life come *from* me , not *at* me.

Acknowledgements

To those who stayed — your light steadied me.
To those who left — your absence sharpened me.
To my mother — I turned loss into language, and silence
into spells.
To every whisper inside that refused to hush — thank
you for surviving me.
To the family I come from and the one I've become —
thank you for the chaos and the calm.
And if you're reading this — you're holding pages that
nearly never made it.

1. I Am My Ma's Echo

Entry *0.04 Hz: the grief never asked me if I was ready*

A shadow walks beside me—
silent,
familiar.
Why is it here?

Silence screams
Haunted
in my dreams.

She was my anchor.
I love her.
A lullaby lives trapped
in my throat,
while I float
in storms she once calmed.

Fading voice, fading scent—
I was her echo,

now static,
crawling frantic,
woke in hell,
Descended when?

I try to hold on—
but it's smoke,
slipping through the hands
that once held hers
without fear.
I scream underwater.
No one hears.

There's so much to say,
but I'm lost in the fray.
How do I get out
when all I can do
is shout?

2. God's Prison on Earth

Entry *3.66 Hz: baptized in gasoline*
I do not *sit with my feelings*
for long these days,
because I don't know
if I will be able to get up.

And if I do—
will I *stay*, or *run*?
Run towards or *away*?

Feelings are the biggest trap,
God's prison on Earth.
Maybe that's why saints give up desires—
because the **fires they start**
are unstoppable.
Unsatisfied by water,
all they desire more is **gasoline.**

And believe me when I say it—
the world has **no shortage** of it.

3. Bittersweet Relief

Entry *3.06 Hz: From Smoke to Salvation*

Smoke is coming,
But from where?
Ashes are falling,
Hell is here?

People are running,
Towards or From?
Chaos is descending,
Like Carrie's Prom?

Wait.
It's coming from me!!
Am I burning?
They are running from me!!

Maybe I should run,
Towards or From?
It could be fun,

Like Carrie's Prom.

Am I burning?
Or being burned?
Like a witch on a stake,
God!! Why is everyone so fake?

Wait.
Who's that?
Running towards me,
Are they come to save or stake me?
God, please make it rain,
And save me from this pain.

I feel better now even though it burns a little,
Bittersweet relief,
I guess I am happy to be alive,
But I have got to learn to whittle,
And let them come with their unpeace,
I guess chaos is where I thrive.

4. That Reason Can't Put Out

Entry *2.22 Hz :Fury and Desire in Equal Measure*

Uncertainty exists—
To only make us crave certainty.
Monotony exists—
To only make us crave adventure.
Expectations exist—
To only make us crave freedom.

Why?
Why can't we simply accept what is given to us?
Why must we dissect in search of everything,
Only to find nothing?

The gods knew the heart was *wild,*
So they put it in a cage.
But it wasn't enough,
And now, nothing will ever be.

Desires start fires,
Difficult to put out.
Something in wires,
Must break out.

Blazing, raging,
Swallowing doubt,
That reason can't put out.

5. The Anatomy Of Apathy

Entry *2.06 Hz : there's no turning back now*

They keep looking for the girl I used to be—
Hoping, praying, begging
for my return.
Loving, caring, empathetic—
are the words they use to describe me with,
or perhaps... used to.

But that girl is gone,
and no amount of
hoping, praying, begging
will bring her back.
I cannot *love,*
I cannot *care,*
I cannot *empathize.*
I will not *feel—*
because I must heal

.

What they see me as now—

uncaring, indifferent, apathetic—
is not a choice, but an obligation.
It is not a cure,
but a prevention.

I cannot give them what they want from me:
love, care, and empathy.
For pain now haunts me,
and all I have now—
is **apathy**.

6. Fire forgives?

Entry *3.12 Hz : when healing smells like smoke*

Standing in ashes,
are they my own?
What I build next,
will it be my own?

Fall and get up,
is what they say.
Something stronger will rise,
every time I break away.

I am tired of burning,
almost feeling,
healing only,
to burn again.

How long before I feel
like chaos is all I have?
How long before I feel

Fire is the only warmth I'll ever have?

If I burn the world then —
Will all be forgiven?

7. Prometheus Lied

Entry *3.33 Hz: To chase cheese and call it purpose*

I have a question.
Is it true damage can be done beyond repair?
Is it true to be broken but not destroyed?
Is it true that everyone wears a mask—
And doesn't know if they can breathe without it?
Is it true to see the light—
But never step into it?

Is it true to suffer more than what was planned for you?
Is it true we go in circles—
Calling it destiny,
Hoping it's not just design?

Inhale to exhale?
Love to lose?
Run to stop?
Hide to be found?
Disguised to be revealed?

Born only... to die?
When the time is "right"?
When the hands finally align?

Well, if that's true—
Then I know why life is called a **rat race.**
Running in circles
To get to the cheese
With the fastest pace.

So if life is a lie—
Then death is...
Truth?
Or just another dare?

8. Flickering

Entry *4.27 Hz* : *flickering but never fully out.*
Exhausted I feel,
But still, I breathe.

Like a flickering flame,
Wondering —
Is it just the wind,
Or am I out of oil,
With nothing left to claim?

Am I depressed,
Drowning in sadness, guilt, and shame?
Or simply *oppressed.*
Wondering —
Is this fate,
Or is there something to be done about me?

And if you were me,
Would you know the difference?
Wondering —

Will I ever know the difference?
Or simply grow indifferent?

9. Reading Ashes

Entry *3.19 Hz* : *To Read Is to Reignite*
Some read
To ignite the dormant fire,
Some read
To reignite the dying flame,
But then —
Some read
To feel the fire.

The fire that burns within them,
The fire they're told burns too bright —
That it might consume them alive.
But that's not the truth.

Year after year,
The world has desensitized itself,
Now scared to evolve into a better self.

It lies to protect its frozen truths,
Afraid their fire might melt them,

And lay those truths —
Bare and blinking in light.

10. Ashes To Nation

Entry *4.16* : *From Smoke We Rise*

The world burned,
Ashes remain.
Yet I still feel this urge,
I must resurge.

People are hurting,
Authorities are smirking.
I must be their source of reliance,
Even if I have to stand in defiance.

Growing incandescence,
Reckoning rise.
To protect the realm's essence,
All truths are on trial,
Clever or Cruel,
We'll summon the fire, we'll break the duel.

It is time for reclamation,
Time to let go of frustration,

Time for investigation,
Time for dedication.
Time to reclaim what's been lost,
No matter the price, no matter the cost.

Let us rise together —
With no fear, no tears,
As one nation,
Hearts ignited, fueled by belief,
A chorus of strength, we'll find relief.

11. You Hated My Rhyming

Entry *4.19* :*Phoenix Taking Names*
Born of ash and flame,
Won't be tamed.
Here I come.
Let the world beware—
It's time to make things clear.

Your polished deeds?
Now broadcasted in everyone's newsfeed.
You better not run,
Cause it's finally about to get fun.

For so long you wore this martyr's hide,
Sorry to cut short your false stride of pride.
Everyone sees you for who you are now,
And don't waste your last seconds of freedom wondering
how.

It is just the beginning,
Wheel is turning,

What a timing,

Right?

And to think all this time you hated my rhyming.

12. What comes next?

Entry 4.23 :*Spirals, Silence & Something*
What comes next?
How should I know.

What comes next?
How would I know.

What comes next?
Stop asking.

What comes next?
What comes next?
Something — I guess.

What comes next?
I don't know.

What comes next?
Anger.

What comes next?
Laughter.

What comes next?
Madness.

What comes next?
Oh stop it!

What comes next?
Why?

What comes next?
Leave me be.

What comes next?
Ahh —

What comes next?
Silence.

What —
Shh —

Everything,
And Nothing,
And Something —

Finally Nothing,

Then Something,
Then Everything.

Yes...?

13. Running With Life

Entry *4.33* : *Awakened & All In*
Something stirs,
Something I haven't felt in a while.

A rush —
A breath without burden,
A heartbeat
A rebirth.

Awoken from sleep,
Nightmares and dreams unravel.
I am awake.
I am alive.

Ready to run,
To fall,
To rise again.
To fight.
To want.
To believe.

Ready to let it out —
Then in —
To begin,
To feel again .

Pushing death back,
Running with life.

Finally —
I am all in.

**Something stirs,
Something I haven't felt in a while.**

14. Class Dismissed (But Never Really)

Entry *4.18:*Those Were the Days

It was 2022, the last time I walked in there.
Now, just a building — a distant memory.
But back then?
It was my home.
The first place where I felt I could be anyone.
Where I mattered not for who I was *to* someone,
But for who I was *becoming.*

Not a background character.
Not another branch on the family tree.
Just a girl finding her own outline,
Learning to color outside the lines.
Not a story already told.
I was the plot twist.
I was becoming me.

Funny how I hated waking up for it,

Six out of seven felt like a grind.
But still,
Still, I showed up.
Still, I lived those years like they mattered —
And maybe they did, they did!

Moving from one grade to the next,
Like unlocking levels in a game.
But when you make it to level 12...
Do you win?

No.

Because that's when you realise —
The *real* game begins.
That was just the warm-up.
The marathon starts *now*.

Time to fold your uniform into your last drawer,
And pick a new one each day,
For whatever role life decides to cast you in.
No more classes,
But lessons —
Every. Single. Moment.

From color-coded timetables
→ to chaos-coded calendars.

From bell rings and recess
→ to alarms and unpaid stress.
From 5 subjects
→ to a hundred uncertainties.

Suspensions are rare in the big house,
And detentions?
Well… life calls that "consequences."
From frolicking in corridors
To walking into meetings,
From dancing at birthdays
To dancing at weddings.

From **"keep the class quiet!"**
To **"keep the world calm."**
From being surrounded by friends
To being surrounded by…
Vipers in disguise.

From planning a timetable
To building a *life-table.*
What a fable!

And you thought adulting was a prize?
More like a puzzle —
You find new pieces every day,
And the day you find the final one?

Game over.
No more moves left.

But every now and then,
I go back.
Open that drawer.
Hold that creased old uniform.
And whisper to myself —
Those were the days.

15. Nevermind, You May Kneel

Entry *4.17Hz* :*Does the Crown Think Too Much?*

Mirror, mirror on the wall —
Why do I think too much?
Or not at all?

Silent storms in my head
make me feel
like a moon in a shadowed sky,
wearing the blackthorn crown.
I must not frown.

They say my questions are knives.
My stories are lies.
But I built a castle
out of every answer they never gave me.
A fortress of what-ifs.
A throne of thorns
carved from things unsaid.

And here,
I rule.

My doubts are dragons.
They taught me how to fly.
My doubts grew claws, not feathers.
My fears — slaves tied in velvet chains.
My rage?
A witch in the tower,
a black swan in a sea of white.
Will they ever get it right?

I am not soft.
I am not simple.
With a storm-touched heart,
inhaling pain, exhaling sacrifice —
but the world still calls it fire.
And my soul? Ice.
With a thorn-laced grin, I say —
Nevermind.

And as for you...
You may kneel.

16. The Inheritance of Her Absence

Entry *3.96Hz:* *The Role I Never Auditioned For*

Dear Ma,

When you left, I didn't just lose you.

I lost the only version of myself that made sense.

The part only *you* knew.

The part that didn't have to be strong all the damn time.

And now?

They expect me to pick up where you left off —

the nurturing, the holding-it-all-together, the quiet

giving.

But I never signed up for this part.

No one asked if I was **ready.**

No one even asked if I was *okay.*

I wasn't.

Still am not.

But I learned quickly that

grief is something you're allowed

only in private,
and only for a moment.

They call me the "woman of the house" now.
Funny how that only means *doing everything*,
and getting nothing in return.
Not help.
Not space.
Not even kindness.

It's like I lost you,
and then I lost the right to even feel it.

They say "therapy helps,"
and maybe it does.
But therapy won't carry the daily weight,
won't still the echo of everyone else's needs but mine,
won't teach the world to be softer with me
just because I've learned to smile through breaking.

I try.
God, I try.

My brother?
Still finding his way, like all of us.

And my father?

Still grieving in his own quiet way —
through long silences and long walks,
through not knowing what to say to me
I guess I know why.

But me?
I don't get to grieve.
I only get expectations.

Sometimes I envy you.
Not because you're gone.
But because **you're done**.
No more proving, no more pleasing,
no more pretending everything's fine.

And here I am —
drowning in their needs,
choking on my own,
learning to swim only because no one else will come in
after me.

They call it "growing up."
But it feels more like *being buried alive* in responsibility.
And still expected to bloom.
Sometimes, I want to scream.
Sometimes, I just want to sleep.
Sometimes, I wish it was me instead.

But then I remember —
you'd hate that.
You'd still want me to fight.
But even you would say:
" Sweetheart, you weren't supposed to grow up all at
once,
you were meant to be held, not just hold."

And yet — here I am.
I've learned now,
the difference between a girl and a woman
isn't age, or wisdom, or a job.
It's the moment she realizes
no one's coming to save her.
It's the moment she *becomes everyone else's safety net,*
even while unraveling herself.

I miss you, Ma.
But more than that,
I miss who I was
when I still had you.

Love,
Your daughter.
Still standing, somehow,

with a crown too heavy and arms still longing to be
held.

37

17. Mixtape at 2 A.M

Entry *741Hz:* *Some nights, the silence sings back.*

It's always around 2 a.m.
The echoes of past grow louder,
asking questions I never had answers to.
My dreams — interrupted by reality's rudeness.
Silent night? *Nah.*
Turns out, it's where all my *too-muchness* goes to
scream.

My pillow's soaked in unsent apologies,
and the ceiling — the only thing that never walks away.
Thoughts drip like leaking faucets.
I can't fix them — I just listen.
Listen to the same story over and over again
with a different ending every time.
How could I have known?

They say if you change the past,
you wouldn't be here today —

but no one asked me if I wanted to be here.
And I never spoke up either.

Regrets are the poison we feed ourselves,
funny how no autopsy ever mentions it.
You know I tried everything,
Even counting sheep —
but they kept morphing into memories.
Even writing letters — though I never send them.
I fold them, keep them under my pillow;
who knows more confessions than my friends ever will.
Or I whisper them to the moon —
she just listens, never judges.

Sleep tiptoes around me,
scared to interrupt the madness.
So I stopped fighting.

I learned to breathe underwater —
they call it anxiety,
I call it a talent no one applauds.
But that's okay.
I prefer silence.
I could certainly use some of it.

I've accepted that it's okay to not be accepted.
Not everyone hears the music

or knows how to dance.
Two left feet and musically-challenged minds
They follow the rhythm — even if it's out of tune.
They march in line. I drift in melody.

As for me?
I'm a mixtape of overthinking
and imaginary scenarios —
played on loop.
Some nights,
I even sing along.

18. Some Knives Come Hidden in Hugs

Entry *3.96 Hz* :*Some betrayals don't stab you in the back,
they hold you close and call it love.*

Some knives come hidden in hugs,
lies swept neatly under the rug.
Sadness turns to cold clarity,
wearing the familiarity of an old friend.
Is this the end?

Some friendships rot quietly,
like fruit left too long in the sun.
We built a bridge between us —
you set it on fire,
still expecting me to swim across.
Challenging me at my worst.
Your loss.

You've been playing victim for so long,
you thought I'd wear the blame,

beg for forgiveness,
crawl for your comfort.
No, madam.
I am done.

Make me your villain —
it's a promotion compared to being
a self-deprecating, aggravating,
loathsome, hypocritical,
insensitive "friend."

I'll wear your blame like armor.
At least it's more honest
than the games you played.

19. Growing Up Is a Scam

Entry 4.17 Hz : *They sold us a dream called adulthood.*
Forgot to mention the nightmares were free.

Ask someone what growing up is,
they'll hand you a brochure —
Stable job!
Marriage!
Retirement plans!
but not the fine print that says:
"Congratulations, you've been tricked into joining a
team you never signed up for."
Growing up feels like getting offered lessons
without even entering the school.

They say I'm a people person.
Maybe I was.
Now, I'm just permanently stuck on **"Do Not Disturb."**
They said I could be anything.
I chose **tired.**

I used to walk around with rose-colored glasses,
until I took them off
and realized the world wasn't a garden —
it was a minefield of red flags.
Sometimes entire red billboards.

And still, somehow,
I go colorblind.

I self-sabotage so often
the world barely gets a turn.
The real world isn't a coming-of-age movie.
It's just coming of age, over and over again, without
credits rolling,
only to have someone move the finish line and say,
"One more lap — for experience."
So I leave them on read
and continue scrolling.

I wish growing up wasn't so hard,
and people would stop acting like a "Get Well Soon"
card.
I wish I didn't feel such new, complicated emotions —
I'd rather stick to the basics: **happy, sad, joy, and pain** —
instead of being drained with unbreakable chains.

I'm not afraid of fighting battles.

I'm just tired of signing up for wars I didn't start.

45

20. The Silence I Wear

Entry 5.28: *I didn't choose silence because I had no words. I chose it because no one deserved them.*

The world loves loud things.
Achievements.
Apologies.
Accusations.
But me? I learned to survive by getting quieter.

Silence is not peace.
It's choosing not to explain yourself anymore.
It's screaming inside a locked chest,
where no one even knocks to ask if you're okay.

One day, when you wake up and realize
The people you would have bled for didn't even notice
you were drowning.
It's growing up and realizing —
you can't outcry the ones who don't care,
can't outplead the ones who made leaving look easy.

I wasn't angry.
Not the loud kind of anger that throws things and breaks
plates.
The other kind of angry:
The kind that sits still,
the kind that burns silently under the skin,
the kind that makes you fold yourself smaller and
smaller
until even your own shadow forgets how much space
you once took up.

I laughed when I didn't feel like laughing.
Answered *"I'm fine"* —
even when my throat ached from swallowing the truth.
Studied with hands that shook from exhaustion.
Smiled through grief so raw —
it left splinters in my lungs.

I leave arguments unfinished.
Messages unread.
Questions unanswered.
Not because I don't have words —
but because not everyone deserves to hear them.

And maybe that was the cruelest part:
The silence wasn't just outside.

It started living inside me too.
Silence isn't weakness.
It's a crown made of all the words I refused to waste.

I am not broken.
I am creating pieces no one will ever find.

21. The Impostor Closing at the Finishing Line

Entry *6.96Hz* : *I taught others how to heal while still trying to bandage my own open wounds.*

They told me to love myself
like it was a simple recipe —
a teaspoon of affirmations,
a sprinkle of gratitude —
but no one mentioned
how heavy the spoon gets
when your hands won't stop shaking.

I feel like an impostor
telling everyone healing is real,
writing while I am still *bleeding,*
handing out candy I haven't even tasted yet,
telling you to rise
while I still crawl through the rubble.

I plead guilty.

Truth be told —
some days loving myself
feels like cheering for a team
that already lost the game.

Survival —
my badge of honor —
feels more like a *counterfeit*,
bought at a cheap motel gift shop.

Every poem I wrote about rising from the ashes?
It's more hope than reality.
Because I've been burned
far more times than I deserved,
and somehow —
I haven't turned to ashes yet.
So how would I even rise?

Sometimes,
I wonder if my armor
is just another form of pretense.
Because what could truly protect me
from life itself?

I am exhausted.
Exasperated.
And God, how I wish life had a **Ctrl+Z.**

But... I haven't surrendered.
I might not have won,
but I still —
do —
as little as I can —
wake up,
get out of bed.
Maybe not into the world,
but at least out of my own grave.

Maybe that's why I feel like an impostor —
because everyone thinks I've got it all in hand.
Maybe the bravest thing I've ever done
was make surviving look easy.

Maybe I'd make a decent actor.
But the ruse is up.
And here I am —
The Impostor
Closing At The Finishing Line —
If there's one.

* 9 7 8 9 3 7 0 9 2 3 9 6 6 *